The Guy's Guide to
LOTS OF
GREAT SEX
(For Women Too!)

LORIN BELLER

Illustrations within Chapters by Marian Merour
Illustrations at the beginning of each chapter by Joe Califano

Printed and bound in the United States of America
ISBN: 978-0-9769558-2-5

DEDICATION

This book is dedicated to

You.

Because

You are taking your precious time to get a glimpse, some insight into the most challenging spiritual path on the planet, and one that should not be taken lightly. Intimate relationships are challenging. They're also most rewarding if you bring your whole self to them— and that's where this journey begins.

ACKNOWLEDGMENTS

I'd like to thank and acknowledge Joe Califano for sharing his great artwork at the beginning of each chapter—reminding us that if we stay in our best, most beautiful selves, our relationships can bloom every day. But even more importantly, he has modeled for me how to be in relationship with humor, consistency, love, kindness, and healthy boundaries as my mother's partner for the past 30+ years. Grateful. I would like to thank and acknowledge Bethany Kelly, my book coach, for partnering with me to take a stale vision and make it come alive in this book. I look forward to many more with you!

PREFACE

This book is written for both men and women. In my 16 years of work supporting thousands of women entrepreneurs (as well as some awe-inspiring men!), I cannot count the many, many times when the challenge that is brought up is the relationship we have with our partners. I think both men and women (all partners) have so much to learn on this topic, sometimes from each other! That is why I wrote this book.

First, it is important to know this about women: for the most part, we want to please, we work hard, we see things that need to be done and do them, and we put others first, sometimes to a fault. We think very differently than men do, but our world needs both types of brains.

I've come to respect both perspectives and both approaches to life. We need both to survive well.

After having so many one-on-one conversations with people about their partners and what it has meant to them to have their partner support them, I felt that it was time to take the gifts of insight I have gained over the years and share them. From what I can see, women's collective vision is that we want to be seen and treated as *partners* in our homes, our offices, and this world. Women want to be respected deeply in all areas of life. We want to live *well* with men, to create a loving, honoring, respectful, fun, adventurous, playful, happy life together. We would like to have partners who are our best friends, yet really know how to turn us on (and I don't mean just sexually). We would like to have partners who realize that we have great gifts that our world needs and who also want us to "go for it" and will have our backs along the way. And we want to have our partners' backs too; we want to be there for you. We already know that it is truly the little things in life that matter. It is the kind, simple acts that at the end of the day, and the end of our lives, will matter most.

I know the above vision is possible, and with this quick and easy guide I hope that we can all move more swiftly into this vision together. Because really . . . life is rather simple. We all complicate it too much.

Cheers to the simple sweetness of life together.

TABLE OF CONTENTS

CHAPTER 1

ACKNOWLEDGMENTS AND CURIOSITY

Acknowledging others is a very simple act that does not come naturally to most people. But if we are open to *learning* along this path and are willing to practice, the skill will come naturally.

Acknowledgments cost nothing!!!

An acknowledgment has two parts:

1. Name/Pet name

2. What you appreciate about someone (try to make it about the person rather than materialistic things)

One simple, heartfelt acknowledgment can change the entire mood of a situation. An acknowledgment raises the energy in a relationship to be loving rather than blah. Acknowledgments create a sense of intimacy, a sense of closeness, as well as a sense of being seen and noticed. This action gets you points whether you are a woman or a man!

Men, think of it this way: The more points you acquire, the more sex you get . . . generally!

For the most part, acknowledgments should be authentic (real and honest). But in relationships, authentic can sometimes be shitty, so rather than be authentic, be kind. My boyfriend is king of this. I tend to just "say it as it is"; therefore what I say can be taken differently than

I intend it. He has a beautiful way of saying something more kindly than I might say it authentically. I apologize more because of it.

Acknowledgments help one to think more kindly and be more kind. Kindness truly helps every relationship be more fun, easy, and productive.

Following are some examples of the many things that you can acknowledge throughout the day.

FOOD/MEALS

Example:

"Hon, this dinner was delicious. I appreciate you taking the time to cook it for us."

Never let your wife's girlfriend be the one to tell her that her stuffing was the best she ever had. It just does not have the same effect. If you love her stuffing, tell her, especially if you want more stuffing in the future!

Example:

"Baby, thank you for getting to the grocery store today during what I know was a crazy day for you."

KIDS

Naturally, women tend to spend more time taking care of the kids—a sad but true fact. It does not have to be like this . . . and if you notice that she is doing the majority of the work, it is a great place for an acknowledgment. You might say:

Example:

"Beautiful, I noticed that you've been doing a lot lately with the kids (baths, making their food, cleaning up after them, doing their laundry and putting it away), and I wanted you to know that I could never do all that and look as great as you do at the end of the day. You work hard, and I appreciate all you do for them and me. You are a great mom and partner. Thank you!"

HOW SHE LOOKS

Whenever you have that thought of "She's cute," or "Oh, she looks nice," or "Wow, she is hot," *say it*!!!! So many times men think it and then go straight for the sexual comment. But stop yourself for a moment and acknowledge her in every way.

Examples:

"Honey, that color looks great on you."

"My sexy thing, I love how your arms look in that photo."

"Sweetness, that night shirt makes you look really cuddly."

"You hot thing, your new haircut has you looking sassy today!"

"Honey, I love going out with you beside me. You look like a million bucks."

HOLIDAY/BIRTHDAY TIME

So, it's holiday time, and she's the shopper of the family, as most women are. You don't need to step foot into a mall or a big box store. You don't need to think about cards for the family. She takes care of all this for you. This is a perfect time and place for an acknowledgment.

Example:

"Babe, I want you to know that I truly appreciate you taking the time and energy toward getting presents for people, and not just at holiday time but all year long. You're very thoughtful and always get great gifts and send them on their merry way with all our names on them. I appreciate you doing that task for me all year long. I know it's a lot of work, and I don't enjoy it. It's a big relief to me that I don't have to do it."

A SIMPLE THANK YOU

Remember, in the beginning of the book we said that women are pleasers . . . Therefore they will often do these very small acts of kindness, like bring you dessert on the couch, that will last if they are acknowledged with simple words of gratitude.

These two simple words can be said over and over again for lots of points: "Thank you."

Plus, it's very good for your kids to hear you say "Thank you" to Mom for doing little (and big) things. It creates thoughtful kids in the world! And God knows, we need more of those!

ACKNOWLEDGMENT: WHAT *NOT* TO DO

MAN: I am putting together a PowerPoint for my presentation at work, and I'm using photos of you and the kids.

WOMAN: Really? Can I see what you are putting together?

MAN: Sure! Here is one of you.

WOMAN: Why do you like that photo of me?

MAN: Because it has the boat in the background. . . .

Part of basic communication is having a strong sense of curiosity about your partner. Being curious about our partner is another way of making them feel seen and heard, because real genuine curiosity feels good! Take a moment to think about how your loved one might be feeling, what they might have done with their day, what is going on with them personally, professionally, as a person, as a parent, as a partner, as a human being. Ask basic questions like:

"What was a highlight from your day today?" (Great family dinner table question!!)

"What was one thing that was frustrating today?" (Again, another great family dinner table question)

"What would be fun for you this weekend?"

"I'd love to hear about the meeting you had today. Will you tell me about it?"

In relationships, when you see that your partner is into something, you often tend to resent it because it pulls them away from you. But the best thing you can do is be curious about whatever it is . . . learn why they love it. Support them in their new interest. We tend to resent, and that drives a wedge between us and decreases our intimacy. Stay honestly curious about their new interest.

CHAPTER 2

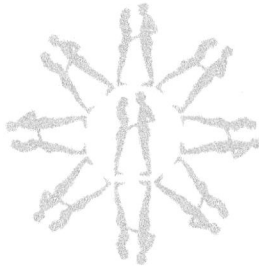

BE A PARTNER

There are a few parts to this step. First, ask this key question often:

"What can I do for you?"

Say you are watching TV or relaxing on an "i-something" (iPhone, iPad, iWatch, or the like), and you wish she'd join you, but she is

hustling and bustling around the house. At this moment when you do not know what you can do for the partnership, *ask*! This perfect question is such a nice thing to hear. When we are overwhelmed, it is nice to know that someone notices that we are overwhelmed—again, seen and heard. Asking our partners "What can I do to help" is a sure sign that we have each other's back. Doesn't that feel better than being criticized?

If you are on your "i-something"—I would like to point out that it is appropriately named: an "i-something," not a "we something"—and if you want more intimacy, then you need to find a "we something" regularly. That could be:

- a conversation
- a game
- an activity
- a project
- the kids
- a topic

Search for more "we somethings"—it will be worth it!

IN THE KIDS DEPARTMENT . . .

Kids are not just her responsibility. They have both mothers and fathers! Take responsibility for your part, identify what your part is going to be, and do it . . . and do it well. Do it with love. (Your child knows the difference, and so does your partner!)

Believe it or not, your child knows if you really want to be doing what you are doing or not. They are brilliant souls who learn more from what we do than what we say.

Plus, women think it is sexy when men are great with kids. And women know the difference between truly doing it because you care and doing it to just *look* like you care.

If you are one of those parents who put your kids before your spouse, your kids need to see you treat their other parent like gold. It is how they learn to choose partners that treat *them* like gold. It is *that* simple.

TRANSPARENCY

If you want to feel like you have a partner and are a partner, it is critical to be *transparent*. What does this mean? Be open, tell her what is on your mind, and *share* about your day without being asked. The more transparent you are, the more we feel connected to you and the more connected we feel you are to us. Being transparent gets you lots of points, because it makes us feel like we are on the team with you. It makes us feel like we are a part of your plans. It makes us feel like we are important to you. After all, women share with those they feel close to.

DO SOMETHING JUST FOR HER

Sometimes do something just for her. Not the kids, not yourself, but for her. These are called acts of service.

Here are some ideas:

- Cook an entire meal for everyone and clean up.
- Plan a night out, get the sitter, make the reservations, and acknowledge her when she comes out and is ready to go.
- Draw a bath for her with candles and a glass of wine, because you can tell she needs and deserves it.
- Do the kids' bedtime when she least expects it.
- When you are sending her an email, be sure to include "a sweet nothing," because you know she will appreciate it. It takes no time and costs nothing! (More on this later.)

Don't expect your partner to do it all. Rudy's (a BBQ restaurant in Austin, Texas) has this sign on its wall: "Your mother does not live here, please clean up after yourself." Some houses need this sign in it!

Most women (and some amazing men!) clean up after everyone. So clean up at least after yourself, and if you really want points, pitch in and just clean up!

A CULTURE OF KINDNESS

Just like every corporate office, a home also has a culture, and every single person contributes to that culture. A culture of kindness is enhanced when every person is kind. When some are kind and one is not, this is seen clearly by those who are being kind and tarnishes the culture in a single moment. This gives every single person lots of power to contribute to the culture or detract from it. Helping create a culture of kindness scores men (everyone!) lots of points! Try it and see what the outcome might be. And when both adults in the household consciously choose kindness as the tone and culture they want for their home and take responsibility to create it, you create a magical home culture.

CHAPTER 3

BE RESPECTFUL

Men tend to flee when it comes to disagreements and hard conversations; they leave, go exercise, or head to the garage.

Women have a very different need—to finish or continue the conversation until it is complete and we all come to a conclusion, a plan, a lesson, a new way next time, etc.

Part of respect is ensuring that everyone's needs are being met.

So, if you have to walk away, do it, but not without the understanding that there is an incomplete conversation that needs to be completed.

Make a point of coming back and deciding when you will *both* be available to complete the conversation. (We will discuss more on the mechanics of this shortly.)

But never walk away with the intent of avoiding the conversation and sweeping it under the rug altogether. This only causes more of a wedge. A great goal is to have no intentional wedges, only intentions of connection.

Another biggie we all do: ASSUME.

Never assume.

This is challenging to do. But again, with practice we get better at it. Assuming gets us all in trouble.

I apologize a lot for my assumptions. If you are making an assumption, check it out. If you sense that you just made an assumption, you can check it out by asking something like, "I think I just realized I might have made an assumption about _____. Is that true?" Or if your assumption creates conflict, clean it up. Discuss. Take responsibility for your part. Apologize.

Why are the words "I'm sorry" so difficult for us to say? Our egos hate being wrong. Honestly, isn't it easier to admit you made a mistake and apologize rather than get or give the cold shoulder for anything more than ten seconds? If we want to avoid that whole drama scene, we need to ditch the ego.

CHAPTER 4

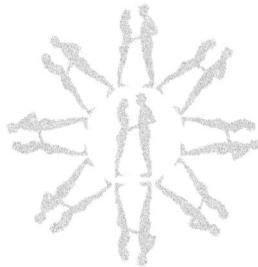

RESPONSIBILITY AND CHOICE

What culture do we really want to create in our home? *We get to choose this!* We tend not to think about the power of the culture in a home. It just sort of happens. But the reality is that when we realize that we choose our culture, we can positively (or negatively) change it just by being aware of it.

The second we blame our spouse for our current state of mind, we are no longer taking responsibility for ourselves.

We have to *both* be willing to commit to being 100% responsible for the energy we bring into the home.

Men are 100% responsible for creating their energy, just as women are also 100% responsible for creating their energy.

So what happens when we fall into a situation where we have a mess between us? A mess can be an issue, misunderstanding, conflict, etc.

I suggest a tool that was shared with me by relationship coach Charles Zook. It is called SQR, which stands for:

Sharing
Questions
Requests

Using this tool helps us to express ourselves during a misunderstanding.

Sharing means making a statement, stating how you feel or a point of view.

After one person shares, the other person acknowledges that you heard her or him say it, stating what you think you heard.

The purpose of a question should be gaining information, and the response to a question is a period of sharing. The only time the response would be a question is if you wanted a clarification about what the question was about. This example may help:

The purpose of a question should be gaining information, and the response to a question is a share. A challenging conversation will be more effective if we don't use questions to diminish the other person or to place blame. Consider the energy of the following scenarios:

SCENARIO ONE, COMMON COMMUNICATION STYLE

Bob: You're late. Are you going to tell me you had car trouble again?

Sam: Are you implying that you don't trust me, Bob?

Bob: What's not to trust?

Sam: What's not to trust? Have you noticed how often you make excuses?

COMPARED TO A MORE SQR-ISH STYLE OF COMMUNICATING

Bob: Sam, you were late for the meeting this morning. What happened? (Question)

Sam: Honestly, Bob, I thought the meeting started at 9:30, not 9:00. (Share)

Bob: I see. You had the wrong start time. (Response to share) Can we talk about what's on my mind? (Request)

Bob's final question is a request. A request is a question that requires someone to take action. In response to a request, you can agree, disagree, or make a counteroffer. In our example, Bob may conclude this conversation by requesting that Sam be on time for subsequent meetings. Sam may agree to be held accountable or not, or he might make a counteroffer by agreeing to at least phone if he is going to be late.

This simple framework might feel clunky at first, especially the part about letting someone know they have been heard before responding with a share or a question or a request. The reward, however, is a true honoring of each other's voice, acknowledging the importance of each other's thoughts, feelings, and opinions, and being able to stay in a powerful place of positive communication rather than creating misunderstandings.

NOTE: I want to thank Charles Zook, an extremely talented relationship coach who was gracious enough to allow me to share his SQR technique. If you have questions about SQR or are in need of a coach for a relationship you are in, please contact him: CZook@CharlesZook.com

OK, let's get back at it!

We cannot do any of this SQR technique if we are not willing to take responsibility for ourselves and our part in our relationships.

When my daughter was two and a half and started preschool, she attended a Montessori school. This is when I learned what the Montessori "peace flower" was. (Some schools have peace tables, some have flowers, some have rocks . . .). When two or more children have a conflict, they use the flower. The children that had the conflict take turns holding the peace flower, and the person holding the flower is the one who gets to speak, while the other's job is to listen. They each state their part in the conflict one at a time while holding the flower. They listen to each other share their part, and then they work to find a solution. I remember my young daughter learning this, and to this day she understands that in any "situation," we all have parts. If we do not think we have a part in a conflict, we are kidding ourselves and walking around with blinders on. And relationships will not change if we keep the blinders on. We need to be willing to look in the mirror and see our part. Drop the ego, be responsible, don't blame, and choose to take responsibility for your part of the situation. When we can do this, we transform relationships.

CHAPTER 5

AFFECTION

One of those amazing men I have worked with for years told me one of his "secrets" to success in his thirty years of marriage. He said: "I touch her all the time. Every time she is within arm's length, I reach out to touch her." He went on to say, "I truly believe this makes all the difference."

Touch her in the kitchen by rubbing her shoulders; let the love that you feel in your heart come through your fingers!

When she walks in the room, how do you feel? You used to love it when she walked into a room. Be curious and look within yourself for what you loved about your significant other walking into a room early on, and try to remember and tell her so using your hands. When someone touches us with love in their heart as opposed to touching us when they are not feeling loving, they are two very different touches.

We can be affectionate in an email too. Let's face it, we email all day long. And when you take three extra seconds to say, "Love you. Miss you," it makes all the difference. Some call them sweet nothings, but I call them "sweet everythings"! You can communicate affection in text messages as well. How nice is it to receive a "sweet everything" in the middle of your busy day?!

A few examples of verbal or text "sweet everythings":

- Thinking of you.
- Looking forward to looking into your eyes tonight.
- I like you.
- You rock (my boat).
- Good afternoon, baby; almost time to see you!

Let's talk a bit more about the type of "sweet everything" touch I am talking about. What I would *not* do is slap her on the butt or grab her boob! This is not the kind of touch I am talking about.

(I also want to say that this gesture can go both ways, ladies! I have had women test this "secret ingredient" of touching their partner whenever he was in arm's length, and I have been told that it's a game changer; they love it! Try it!)

"Sweet everythings" *are free, cost nothing*, and have a huge impact.

CHAPTER 6

GET OVER YOUR EGO—YOU DESERVE IT

actually hate the word *deserve*. We live in an entitled world, and that's a problem. We think we deserve so much. But really, we are responsible for what we want. Ask yourself: Did I take responsibility for earning what I want?

I suggest we come to terms with the question: "What did I do to earn my spouse's respect, love, and kindness today?"

Make your love come alive today or it is not alive! Wait for nothing—no-thing!

What did you do to earn lots of great sex today?

Oh, and by the way, foreplay to women is everything you can implement in the previous five chapters. Foreplay does not start five minutes before sex. So, if you want great sex often, think about using one of the preceding steps about once an hour. Each time you think about sex, choose one of the preceding steps. Do it authentically, from your heart—we know the difference.

So many times we all get frustrated with each other and we do not "return to love." We don't talk through a situation so that both parties feel they can return to love. Forgive.

We must have strong egos to forgive. You have to get over yourself and want to have the best relationship more than you want to be right. Or more than getting your ego stroked. Needing your ego stroked actually costs you your happiness.

I love the saying: "Do you want to be right or happy? You choose!"

I choose happy. Which means I have to let many things go. But I don't mean letting myself be taken advantage of. That's not the point at all. This is probably the most confusing part of a relationship: the point where you try to figure out the boundary between taking care of yourself and letting go of things your partner is doing that irk you. I cannot define your boundary, just like you cannot define mine. But I can say that when you start to notice that you are resenting, mostly likely you have allowed a boundary to be crossed and have not protected your own boundary. This is a fine line, and one that's difficult to define. There have been books written just on this topic. What I have come to know is that if we avoid conflict, we always end up in a mess. And if we are clear about our boundaries for ourselves, we have fewer conflicts and less resentment as well. And only you get to decide where your boundaries are. Generally, the healthier our boundaries, the happier we all are.

CHAPTER 7

IN-LAWS

President Barack Obama said it best in an interview as president-elect: "I do not tell my mother-in-law what to do."

Never, ever, try to tell your mother-in-law what to do. And even more important, never put down in-laws to your spouse. Your spouse can speak negatively about their parents. Your job is just to listen. This is critical to your relationship. Bad-mouthing your partner's parents does nobody any good.

If you cannot be kind, go for a walk, a bike ride, or do what you must to remain kind and keep your boundaries intact.

If you are divorced, hopefully you know the detriment to your relationship with your child if you speak negatively to them about their other parent. This will only cause problems between you and your child. This is exactly the same as speaking negatively to your spouse about their parents. We are created equally by our parents and only we get to decide our relationships with them; nobody else.

We also get to choose our relationship with our in-laws. This is where we often need to have very healthy boundaries for ourselves and learn to be kind before being right.

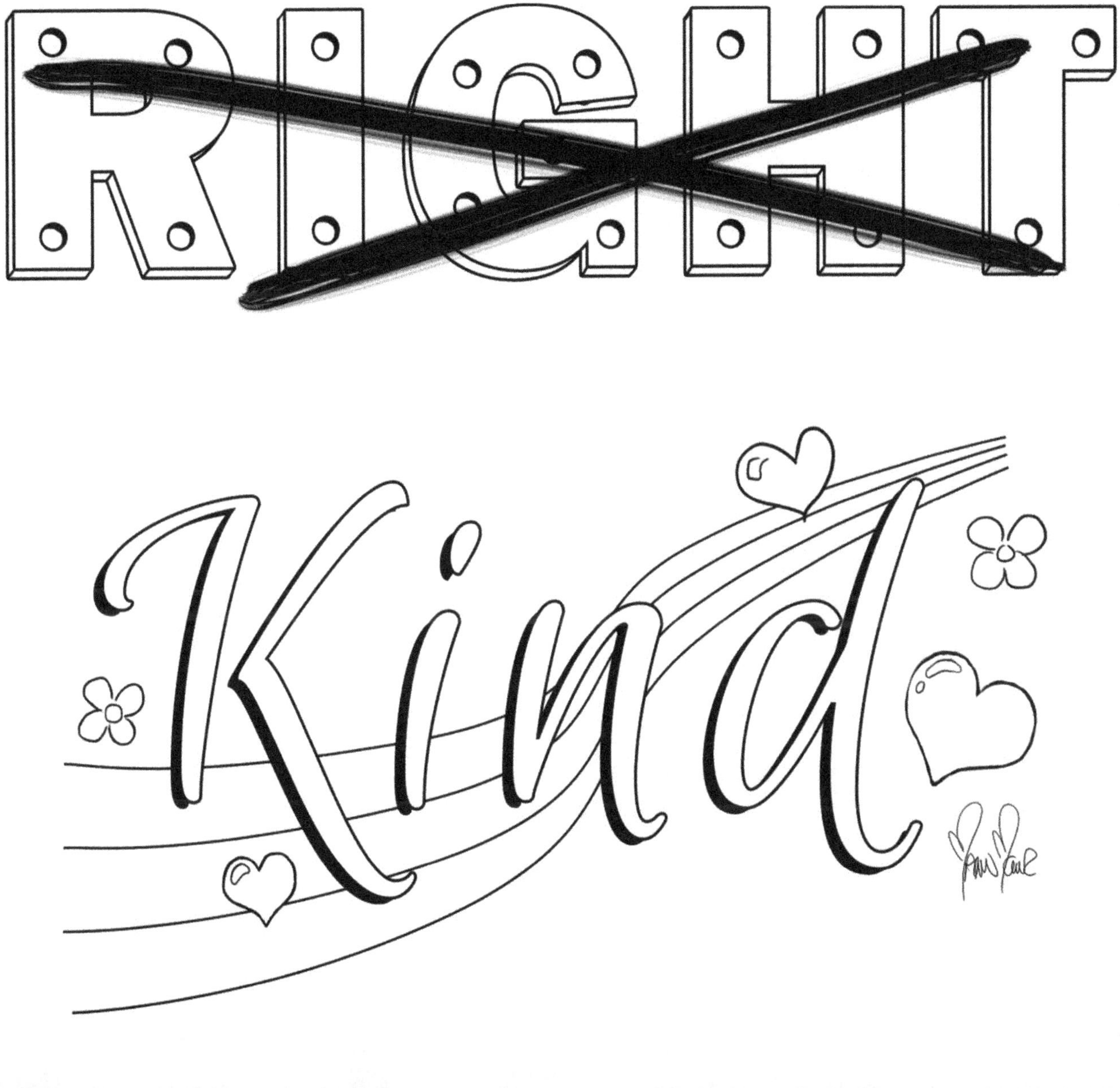
RIGHT
Kind

CHAPTER 8

GIFTS

Some women are all about gifts. They love receiving flowers. They enjoy the surprise of a little box now and then. I don't want to imply that I don't enjoy gifts now and then, because I do.

One guy I worked with said that he gave gifts in categories: music, jewelry, flowers, food, candy, and clothing. But he also said you never give gifts for the kitchen, cleaning, kids, or the car. He was a great gift-giver.

Other women prefer that their men spend *time* with her. They would like a date night. But do you know what is more important than a date night? Taking ten minutes to have an eye-to-eye conversation together, or working on a project together.

I was cooking in the kitchen, and my daughter, who was about six years old at the time, was sitting on the counter talking to me. I was focused on cooking, but very much listening to her. My daughter said, "Stop, Mommy! Come here." She grabbed my face with her little hands on my cheeks and said, "Mommy, listen to me with your eyes."

This is as true for adults as it is for children. We want to be heard. And how we hear each other is by looking into each other's eyes and giving the gift of listening. I like to call it "i-listening."

I believe that we all want to be listened to with our eyes even more than we want to receive gifts.

Just a side note about eye contact: Did you know that in Europe it is often said that if you don't keep eye contact while toasting, it can lead to seven years of bad sex? That's a myth. What is not a myth is that when we toast (with wine or water or apple juice), the proper way to do so is not to look at the glasses but into the eyes of the person you are toasting. What a nice way to make the gesture much more intimate.

What is most important, however, is the consistent "gift of your eyes" in your relationship with your partner.

CHAPTER 9

FOR WOMEN ONLY: OUR PART

First, women, all the previous chapters are for you too! If he can do these things, you can too!! Remember modeling?!?! We all learn from each other. We learn how to be and we learn how *not* to be.

Here are a few things specifically for women:

Acknowledgment: Sometimes you have to ask for acknowledgment. If you do this every now and then, it helps your man know when you like acknowledgments. After three or four times in a certain area, he will start (you would hope) to realize that this area is a great place for acknowledgments. This is called training. Have patience. Some of us are slow learners.

(Unless one is stubborn, stupid, personality-disordered, or does not want to get much use from his penis.)

Curiosity: We need to be curious too. It feels good when someone cares enough to ask and then truly listen to the answer. Be authentically curious!

You also want to teach your kids how to be curious. Tell them: "Hey, Mama needs to be asked today, 'How are you feeling?'" Or, "How did your race go today?" Or, "Do you need any help?" Your kids need you to show them how to be curious and how to ask questions. Do this in front of your spouse now and then. We all need a little reminder.

Partnership: Remember that your partner cannot read your mind. He cannot know what you need, so *ask for help*!! When you do this, you help him to know where you want help. Asking for help may sound like this:

"Could you please pick up dinner?"

"Could you please make me a drink?"

"Could you please do the bedtime routine with the kids tonight?"

"Could you please stop at the grocery store on your way home to pick up some things for dinner?"

And so on.

And remember to say a sincere *thank you* when they agree to do *something,* and then say it again when it is done. *Thank you.* This is a partnership!

Respect: Ask yourself, "What do I need to ask him so that I can better understand his perspective?" When we understand each other's perspectives, we judge less. The moment we judge, we lose respect. Find a new perspective. This is often what we rely on our girlfriends for: to give us a fresh perspective. Also, surround yourself with people who *encourage* you to have respect for your husband, not *discourage* your respect for him. Who we choose to hang with affects us in every way.

Responsibility and choice: You have just as much responsibility and choice in making your relationship and life together rock. Take it! Don't wait for it.

The biggest thing I know that we have responsibility for is the energy we bring to the relationship. Do you remember at the beginning of a relationship when your energy was high, bubbly, happy, bouncy, light, and fun?! *Bring that energy to your relationship.* Don't save it for the cute coach at the gym! Or the neighbor's husband down the street, or the new guy in the office. This is how affairs start. We allow a new interest to bring out our best. And we then blame our spouses that "they are boring or not interested or too busy." The truth is, he hasn't changed; *you have*! So if you want to like who you are in the relationship, *be that person* and do not let your spouse or your kids or in-laws influence the amazing *you*. Show up the way you want to. Don't change because someone else is not being who you want them to be! This is blaming, and it's not taking responsibility for yourself.

Affection: You can reach out and touch too. I had a female client try this, and she said it pulled her out of her comfort zone, and her husband was in heaven. What a simple way to create a husband in heaven . . . and now he wants to please you too. Imagine the change in dynamic with just this change in behavior.

You deserve it. Get over your ego: You also have an ego. We all do. Again, do you want to be right or happy? It's your choice every day. This does not mean you allow yourself to get walked on. It does not mean you walk on others. It means you know your lines in the sand. As Kenny Rogers sings: "Know when to hold 'em and know when to fold 'em."

In-law rules: The preceding rules about in-laws go for you too . . . never ever criticize your partner's parents. They are his parents; they are what he is made of. My boyfriend once told me: "My parents showed me more about how *not* to be than how *to* be." This is a wise perspective. This is exactly why we need to be respectful to all—because we can learn from every person on this planet. Some people teach us how to be and some people teach us how not to be.

Gifts: Material stuff is overrated. Know that. Rise above it. Make your relationships more valuable than stuff. Give the gift of your eyes, your heart, and your time—daily. You are the gift. Give a little bit of you every day. But in order to do this, you have to take care of yourself in every way: spiritually, physically, and emotionally. If we do not fill ourselves up, we cannot fill others up. And we cannot rely on others to be the only ones filling us. We need to take responsibility for taking care of ourselves. That way we can be our best selves toward the ones we love.

BONUS (FOR ALL)

HUMOR

When I refer to humor, I don't mean laughing at people or watching a comedy show. What I mean is having the ability to laugh at ourselves, at the chaos life dishes out now and then, and having the ability to allow others to laugh with us when we make mistakes.

You know those great belly laughs? Life can sometimes be so absurd, the best thing to do is to laugh. And being with a partner you can laugh with is one of the most bonding aspects of a relationship.

And it is excellent to be able to laugh at misunderstandings.

My mother and her husband/boyfriend of 30+ years have a great story. They were driving together. The driver (my mother) said to Joe (the passenger and husband), "Is it okay to move over?" (into another lane; she was asking about his side of the car and wanted him to check to be sure it was safe to change lanes). He said, "Yes, after the bread truck." She said, "I don't see a red truck." He said, "Yes, the bread truck!" She said, "Where is the f!*%ing red truck?!" He said, "*Not Red, Bread*!!!" They were able to burst out laughing at stupidity of the conflict and frustration. When they have similar misunderstandings now, all they need to do is say *Red Truck,* and they both burst out laughing. Not at each other, but at the situation. It immediately dissolves the frustrations and has them laugh *together.*

One of you has to be able to switch to humor in the heat of the moment. And you are BOTH responsible for doing that. I have

something similar with my daughter. When she and I feel ourselves getting frustrated with each other, my daughter is the one that often says, "CAaaaaaalllllllllmmmmmmm Doooowwwwwwwnnnnnn, Mommy." Or I say, "BRRRREEEEEEEEAAAAAAATHHHHHe, MYDAUGHTERSNAME!!!" (I use her real name.) And we both burst out laughing. It works! I am not sure where those words or lines came from, but we have been doing it for years. It breaks the cycle of the heat of the moment and creates laughter for us *both together*.

CHAPTER 10

AN APOLOGY FROM LORIN AND MY CALL TO YOU

I'm sorry. I'm sorry because the title of this book might now seem like I misled you. It was not my intent. My intent was to meet you where you were: your desire before you read this book. And if you picked up the book and are reading this because of the title, it worked, and I hope you got something from it that will help you make your relationship awesome. But as you can see, there are no juicy sex tips.

From my perspective, though, every page is filled with them. Sex is part of a relationship, and it has its own journey—one in which you must be vulnerable, be free. To me, being in an intimate relationship is one of life's greatest challenges. Growing and getting older with someone and being able to see the lines in their face grow from laughter, joy, sadness, and all of life is one of the greatest gifts of our lifetime.

When we find that person we want to watch our lines grow with, it means looking inward a lot. That journey is one only we can decide to be committed to or not, because it is a journey first with ourselves, then with the other person.

What I am talking about has nothing to do with marriage. As a matter of fact, I am not a fan of marriage. I have done it twice. I prefer to wake up each day and decide if I want to be my best self in the relationship or not. Independent from how the other person is being. That is not a commitment to the other person. It is first of all a commitment to myself. From there, we design and redesign our relationship together all the time.

What I also know is that it is only *in* relationship that we learn about ourselves.

And it is only by ourselves that we decide who we want to be, authentically and honestly, and we make a commitment to ourselves to be that person *in relationship*. I like to think of each of us as a "Wild Child of God." And if we choose to evolve spiritually, personally, professionally, as a parent, as a partner—and allow that wild child to live and live fully . . . That, my friend, is pure bliss. Because now you are fully responsible for you and your part of every relationship.

It is such an honor to get to work with so many leaders (Wild Childs!) who allow me to be in their lives in a way that I get a glimpse into their whole life and can create wild success.

Namaste.

ABOUT THE AUTHOR

Lorin Beller has been working with amazing men and women as a life and business strategist for the past 17 years. Lorin has come to learn that success is not success without deep and meaningful connections to those we care most about. This little guide is a compilation of tips that worked well for some people and ways of interacting that do not work at all. It is with great humor and a gentle nudge to be a bit kinder that Lorin shares these tips, because our relationships matter. Why not make them extraordinary? For more about Lorin, see: www.lorinbeller.com

www.ingramcontent.com/pod-product-compliance
Lightning Source LLC
Chambersburg PA
CBHW080147310326
41914CB00090B/893